Floral
Coloring Book

Floral
Coloring Book

ARCTURUS

ARCTURUS

This edition published in 2016 by Arcturus Publishing Limited
26/27 Bickels Yard, 151–153 Bermondsey Street,
London SE1 3HA

ISBN: 978-1-78599-007-6
AD004813NT

Printed in the United States

INTRODUCTION

Coloring is one of the most relaxing and rewarding of pastimes. Use the images of flowers and leaves in this book to produce your own beautiful artwork and patterns with colored pencils. Try to give your images either a harmonious or strongly contrasting combination of colors. Remember to think about tone—this can make the difference between a vivid, strong picture and a subtle, pale result.

Pencil color is not as intense as paint, so it really helps to add layers. When using darker shades, work over the same area several times to produce a greater intensity of color. When making blue or red, for example, add layers of different blues and reds to increase the intensity. Sometimes the addition of purple can give a blue or a dark red more power in the composition. Other times, your top layer can be put on quite lightly, just to change the quality of the color a little.

Try varying the tonal marks of the pencils—cross-hatching, zigzagging or spiraling—to give your finished artwork an interesting texture. As your confidence grows, you will become quicker and more expert and will soon have a portfolio of fantastic floral images to treasure.

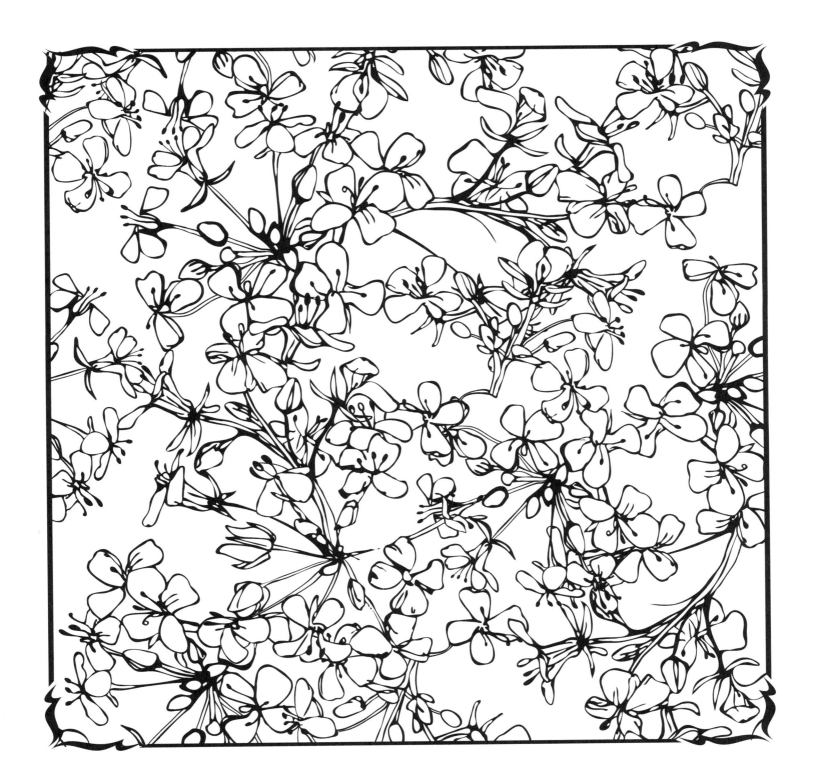

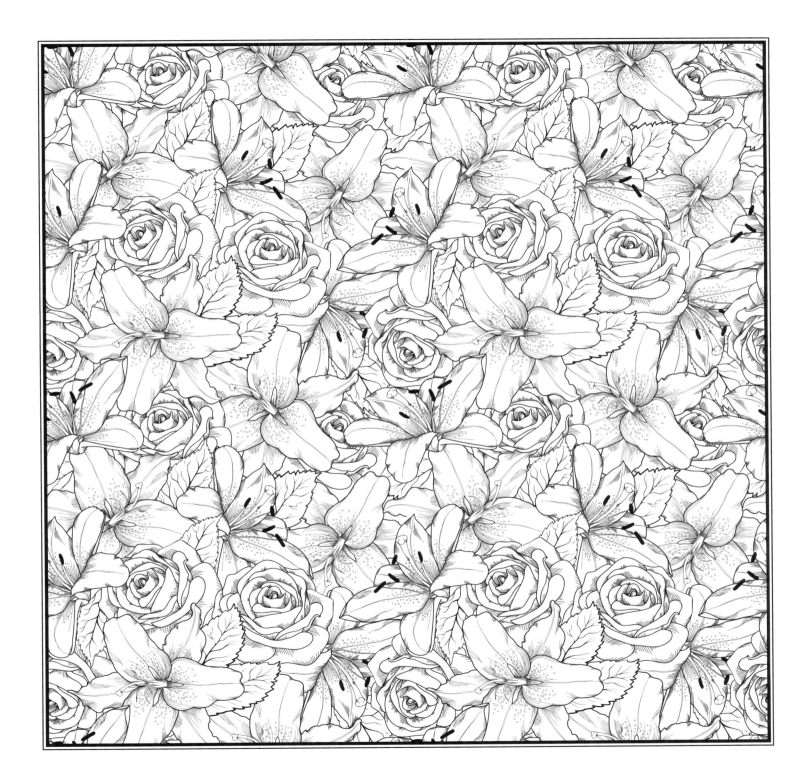

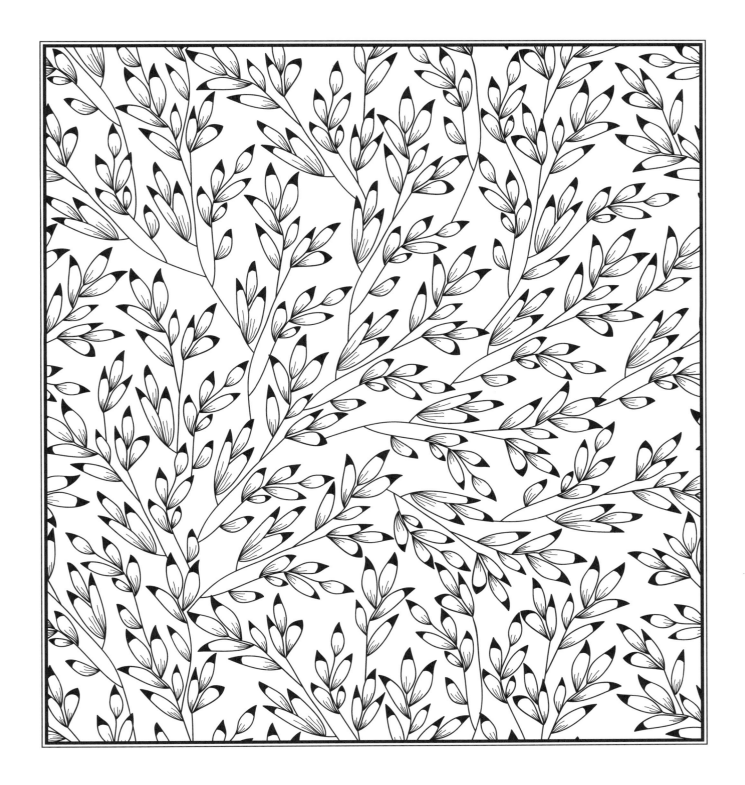

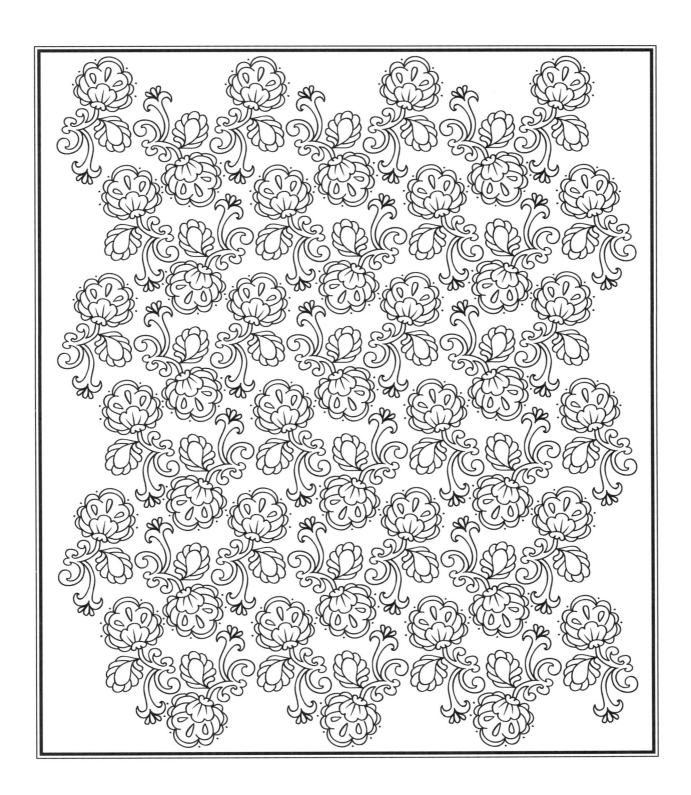

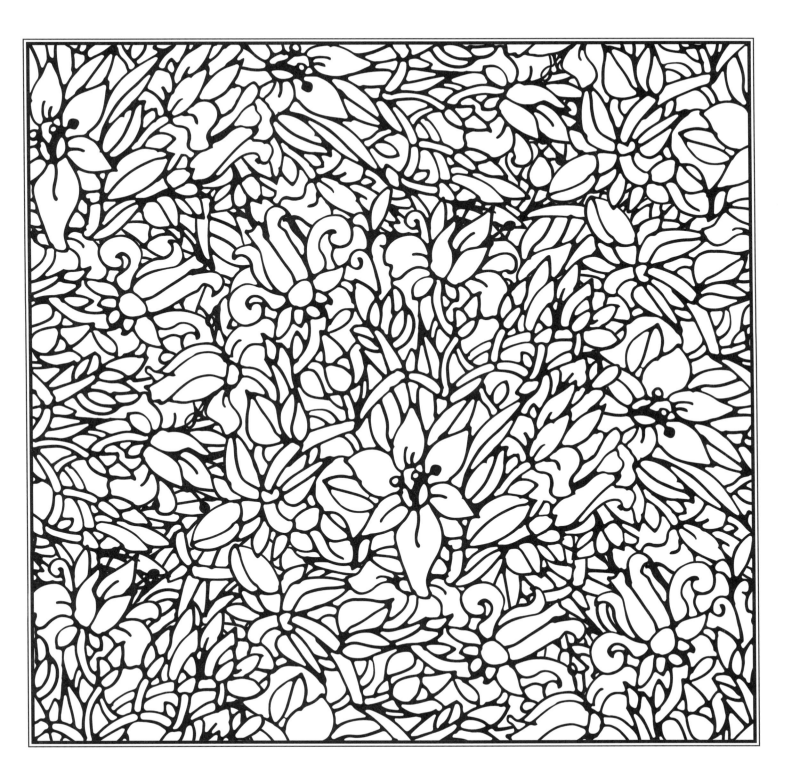